Christian Marriage and Divorce

THE VOICE OF HOLY SCRIPTURE

By
LESLIE S. B. HYDE

GOSPEL STANDARD TRUST PUBLICATIONS
1993
12b Roundwood Lane, Harpenden, Herts. AL5 3DD
ENGLAND

© Gospel Standard Trust Publications 1981

ISBN 0 903556 63 4

First edition 1981
Second edition 1993

Printed in Great Britain at Flair Press, Northampton

INTRODUCTION

Entry upon the marriage state is the most important step that any man or woman may take in his or her life. It has far-reaching consequences and common observation tells us that, though mutual happiness is the intended end, this is not always realized. Where a breakdown in marriage occurs, the reason can often be traced to a lack of understanding of what is involved—the sacrifices that each person contracting has to make; the responsibilities that have to be assumed. Then, again, is the love of each sufficiently deep to withstand the rude shock of realizing that in the past each pleased himself or herself, but now it is a question of pleasing each other, and sharing a life together? Further, the solemnity of the vows taken at the marriage ceremony is not always felt and sometimes marriage is entered into lightly, with no desire or concern to enter upon this new life seriously.

The purpose of this little book is to bring some serious thinking to marriage itself in the light of Scripture teaching, going a little more deeply into the innermost meaning of the marriage vows. How many would have to confess that they had not bothered to consider the subject in depth, or even just a little more than superficially, if asked to offer a few thoughts on the theme?

Broken marriages alas! are on the increase and should produce a cause for deep concern. So a second purpose is to bring forth Scripture teaching on the important matter of divorce. Many opinions have been expressed regarding this, whether there are any grounds for it or grounds for separation temporarily or permanently.

Christian Marriage and Divorce

Then again if such is allowed, is either of the parties concerned given a right to remarry? In looking a little into this apparently perplexing subject, *it is surprising what men have read into the Scriptures in order to support their expressed opinions.*

However, with the help of God, it is not my purpose to express yet a further opinion but rather to state clearly what is contained in the Word of God for do we not read, 'Let God be true, but every man a liar' (Romans 3. 4)?

We shall particularly keep in mind the words of Paul in writing to the church at Ephesus (5. 32): 'This is a great mystery: but I speak concerning Christ and the church.' This will put marriage in its grandest and most attractive form to every true follower of Jesus Christ, every true believer.

Lastly, the great question as to whether a person divorced or living in an adulterous way should be received into church membership or should continue in membership. The point is added because of its importance and the issues which can develop if such cases are not dealt with scripturally.

May the Lord Almighty bless what shall now be written to the benefit of many and especially for the edification of the church of the living God.

CHAPTER 1

MARRIAGE

Its Holy and Sacred Aspect

In this present age of spiritual decline, the true value of many things that are precious is lost sight of. Examples are readily available: to name two, the Bible and Matrimony. Is anything missing? Only one word—'holy'; but what a difference this makes! If it were common practice always to refer to the Scriptures as the 'Holy Bible' (as it is written on the title-page of the Book itself), would it not perhaps produce an awareness in the mind and conscience of people of the sacredness of the Book, that it has to do with God? Likewise, if marriage were referred to as 'Holy Matrimony' (as described in the Marriage Service) whenever reference was made to it, might not the hope spring up in one's mind that it would be a reminder to all that there is a sacredness attaching to marriage, and that it has to do with God?

Various people may be heard to ask such questions as, 'How old is marriage?' 'When was it first introduced?' 'Who thought of it?'. In this degenerate age, ignorance of the origin and antiquity of marriage is amazing; none the less it is sadly true. Marriage was first brought about by the Almighty God Himself. Let us read from the Holy Bible from the Book of Genesis chapter 2 and verses 21 to 24: 'And the Lord God caused a deep sleep to fall upon Adam and he slept: and he took one of his ribs, and closed up the flesh instead thereof; and the rib, which the Lord God had taken from man, made he a woman,

and brought her unto the man. And Adam said, This is now bone of my bones, and flesh of my flesh: she shall be called Woman, because she was taken out of Man. Therefore shall a man leave his father and his mother and shall cleave unto his wife: and they shall be one flesh.'
From this we find that marriage itself goes back before sin entered into the world, when the whole atmosphere and environment of the earth was holy and sacred. Hence marriage in its antiquity and origin may be said to be both holy and sacred, the Almighty God Himself joining Adam and Eve together in a tie that was never dissolved. 'What therefore God hath joined together, let not man put asunder' (Matthew 19. 6).

Are you in the married state? Do you contemplate entering into it? Have you realized the grand and noble beginning of it? Do you behold the beauty of it in its original and find something moving in you that admires God's order? It is feared that many who have engaged in marriage or who contemplate it have given little thought to these things and thus go through a ceremony without realizing its solemnity or that it is professedly taking place in the sight of God, even though their attention is drawn to it in the Marriage Ceremony.

Neither in the Old Testament nor in the New Testament have we any clear indication as to the form a Marriage Service should take. What is in present usage is traditional in its form though agreeable to Scripture teaching in its admonitions, etc. Even so, where a couple profess to be Christians, a church or chapel service would surely be preferred to the legal form conducted at a Registry Office. To seek the Lord's blessing and join in thanksgiving to God is surely very desirable.

Marriage

The Form of the Solemnization of Holy Matrimony

Let us now look more closely at the Marriage Service necessary when a man and woman are joined together in holy matrimony in a right and proper way. This starts off: 'We are gathered together here *in the sight of God* and in the presence of these witnesses to join together this man and this woman in holy matrimony; which is an honourable estate instituted of God in the time of man's innocency (Genesis 2. 22, 24), signifying unto us the mystical union that is betwixt Christ and His church (Ephesians 5. 32, 33); which holy estate Christ sanctioned and honoured with His presence and first miracle in Cana of Galilee (John 2. 1-11); and is commended of the Apostle Paul to be honourable among all men (Hebrews 13. 4): and therefore is not by any to be taken in hand unadvisedly, lightly or wantonly to satisfy men's carnal lusts and appetites like brute beasts that have no understanding* (Psalm 32. 9); but reverently, discreetly, advisedly, soberly and in the fear of God: duly considering the causes for which matrimony was ordained.'

In the Sight of God

The first point of great importance to receive consideration is that this ceremony takes place 'in the sight of God'. We are reminded from the Epistle to the Hebrews 4. 13, 'Neither is there any creature that is not manifest in his sight: but all things are naked and opened unto the eyes of him with whom we have to do.' The eyes of the Lord are penetrating and may be said to be 'a discerner of the thoughts and intents of the heart'. This should

* Church of England Prayer Book Service.

bring into the hearts of the couple to be united a solemn awe when realizing that God not only listens to their words but is aware of the sincerity (or lack of sincerity) of such utterances. Witnesses are also required to be present to testify to the solemn oaths taken.

Instituted of God

'As for God, his way is perfect' (Psalm 18. 30). How clearly is this brought forth in the institution of marriage by God in the time of man's innocency, that is, before man's fall when sin entered into the world! It made the union of man and wife honourable before God and also before men. Are we not all satisfied when we see a man and woman married that not only are legal requirements met, but also the future life of both can be carried on honourably as they live together?

Not to be Entered into Lightly

Where there is true love holy matrimony will not be entered into lightly or unadvisedly. Some marriages that break down are the result of the satisfying merely of 'carnal lusts and appetites like brute beasts that have no understanding'.* There is much more to being joined in marriage than the satisfying of sexual desires; this is but a small part, indeed a very small part of the married state. Where the couple joined together are godly, they will wish to enter upon this great and far-reaching event in

* Church of England Prayer Book Service.

Marriage

their lives 'in the fear of the Lord'. The Holy Bible brings before us what the fear of the Lord is:

1. 'And unto man he said, Behold, the fear of the Lord, that is *wisdom*; and to depart from evil is understanding' (Job 28. 28).

2. 'The fear of the Lord is the beginning of wisdom' (Psalm 111. 10).

3. 'The fear of the Lord is to hate evil; pride, and arrogancy, and the evil way, and the froward mouth, do I hate' (Proverbs 8. 13).

These are just a few Scripture references; there are a number of others, but these are sufficient to show the benefit of this blessing.

Reasons for Holy Matrimony

1. 'It was ordained for the procreation of children to be brought up in the nurture and admonition of the Lord' (Ephesians 6. 4). Hence we have the voice of Scripture speaking to us: 'And God blessed them and God said unto them, Be fruitful and multiply' (Genesis 1. 28); also Genesis 8. 17; 9. 7; 35. 11; Psalm 128. 3). In the aged Paul's first epistle to his son in the faith Timothy, he says: 'I will therefore that the younger women marry, bear children, guide the house, give none occasion to the adversary to speak reproachfully' (5. 14).

2. 'It was ordained to avoid fornication; that such persons as have not the gift of continency might marry, and in this particular keep themselves undefiled members of Christ's body' (1 Corinthians 7. 2, 9).

Christian Marriage and Divorce

3. 'It was ordained for the mutual society, help and comfort that the one ought to have of the other, both in adversity and prosperity.' 'And the Lord God said, It is not good that the man should be alone: I will make him an help meet for him' (that is, suitable to him) (Genesis 2. 18).

So far the minister has set out before the man and woman the meaning and prime purpose of marriage, leaving them without excuse as to what is involved. The points may be summarized as follows:

1. The solemnity of the step they are about to take.

2. The blessing of God rests upon a true union.

3. The Lord Jesus by His personal attendance at the wedding in Cana of Galilee sanctions it.

4. The sober approach to it.

5. The due consideration to be given to the reasons for marriage and the benefits accruing from such a step.

CHAPTER 2

MARRIAGE

Closeness of the Bond of Marriage

This is not such as is described on a piece of paper; neither is it a mere physical attraction; neither can it be said to be that which is spiritual. What is it then? How do the Scriptures describe the closeness of this unity? 'For this cause shall a man leave his father and mother, and shall be *joined* unto his wife, and they two shall be *one flesh*' (Ephesians 5. 31).

Jesus, the Son of God, answering the Pharisees said, 'Have ye not read, that he which made them at the beginning made them male and female, and said, For this cause shall a man leave father and mother, and shall cleave to his wife: and they twain shall be one flesh? Wherefore they are no more twain, but one flesh. What therefore God hath joined together, let not man put asunder' (Matthew 19. 4-6). Can there be a union closer than this anywhere or in anything on the earth? Surely not. Ask the devoted husband whose wife is now dead, or the loving wife whose husband is now deceased, and listen to their spontaneous answer: 'I am bereft of part of myself', or words of similar import. And is the bond only of the flesh? Is it not body and soul? and are not both bound together with love? 'And above all things put on charity which is the bond of perfectness' (Colossians 3. 14). 'Love is strong as death; jealousy is cruel as the grave. . . . Many waters cannot quench love, neither can the floods drown it' (Song of Solomon 8. 6, 7). How pleasant a sight it is to discover a clear witness to a true union, not only as expressed by the lips but as evidenced practically in their lives. Such occasions as silver, golden, or even diamond wedding celebrations often produce statements soberly supporting the strength of the marriage ties.

What is Required of Thee, O Man?

'Wilt thou have this woman to thy wedded wife, to live together after God's ordinance, in the holy estate of matrimony? Wilt thou love her, comfort her, honour her in sickness and in health: and forsaking all other, keep thee only unto her *so long as ye both shall live*?'

What a thrill must course through the woman as she hears the man say in firm tones, 'I will'! A sense of security begins to arise on her horizon. But to look more deeply into the words uttered. The couple and the witnesses in the congregation are reminded of the sacredness of the service and that God's (not man's) ordinance is being carefully observed.

Wilt Thou Love Her?

What is the voice of the Holy Bible? 'Husbands, love your wives, and be not bitter against them' (Colossians 3. 19). 'Husbands, love your wives, even as Christ also loved the church, and gave himself for it. . . . So ought men to love their wives as their own bodies. He that loveth his wife loveth himself. For no man ever yet hated his own flesh; but nourisheth it and cherisheth it, even as the Lord the church' (Ephesians 5. 25, 28, 29). 'Nevertheless let everyone of you in particular so love his wife even as himself' (Ephesians 5. 33). The believer has brought to his attention continually the example of the Lord Jesus Christ as His love respects the church, His bride, and also as he loves himself, with the same intensity is he to love his wife.

Wilt Thou Comfort Her?

'Let the husband render unto his wife due benevolence' (1 Corinthians 7. 3). If this is rightly and feelingly to be given, then whatever the circumstances requiring this comfort, the husband must be so knit to his wife's heart that the sorrow she feels affects him in the same way; whatever injury she sustains he feels the force of it too. In the case of true believers, what comfort will be received when the husband, at the family altar, is able to commit the matter to their loving Lord 'who comforteth us in all our tribulation' (2 Corinthians 1. 4)!

Comfort is conveyed sometimes by words, sometimes by actions; how real is such comfort when words are supported by actions! In Isaiah 40. 2 we read the words, 'Speak ye comfortably', and again in Hosea 2. 14. The marginal rendering of the same scripture is very instructive: 'Speak *to the heart*', or *'friendly'*. How necessary it is to regard this point when pondering, 'Wilt thou comfort her?'

Wilt Thou Honour Her?

'Likewise, ye husbands, dwell with them according to knowledge, giving honour unto the wife, as unto the weaker vessel, and as being heirs together of the grace of life' (1 Peter 3. 7). To discover the source of this we must go back to the Garden of Eden when the Lord God spoke to Adam and Eve immediately following their fall from innocency and uprightness: 'Unto the woman he said, I will greatly multiply thy sorrow and thy conception: in sorrow thou shalt bring forth children; and thy desire shall be towards thy husband, and he shall rule over thee' (Genesis 3. 16). However people in this degenerate age may attempt to deny this, discredit it, abolish it, yet many many women will know in their hearts that this is true: their desire is towards their husband, and he does rule over them. Such rule is not tyrannical or despotic but such as becomes the governing force of love to the weaker vessel. This will include acknowledging her qualities, especially if she is that gracious woman that retaineth honour (Proverbs 11. 16). The Scriptures bring forth an important question and then give the answer: 'Who can find a virtuous woman? for her price is far above rubies. The heart of her husband doth safely trust in her, so that he shall have no need of spoil', etc. But read the rest of chapter 31 in the Book of Proverbs. The general inference is to her industry and attention, which if her husband sees, he will feel not only duty-bound but love-bound to honour her.

Mutual Vows

Marriage vows which are acceded to by both parties may be said to be three, and each one sets forth solemn responsibilities and gives solemn assurances:

1. 'And keep him/her in sickness and in health.'

2. 'And forsaking all other keep thee only unto him/her.'

3. 'So long as ye both shall live.'

Marriage

Hence we have here expressed the complete agreement of the two parties to stand by each other whatever the prevailing and changing conditions of life (in sickness or in health); forsaking all other things or persons, and that until death intervenes. It is clear now to all that the avowed purpose and intention of both husband and wife is to care for each other under all conditions, at all times and in all places, and not to allow the most trying circumstances to produce any reason for separation; forsaking all other to whom either party might have felt drawn earlier, cleaving to one another, eyeing one another with that single eye of love and affection.

So Long as ye both Shall Live

This third point deserves special attention. Can anything be more clear as the expressed sincere desire of each heart that the marriage is purposed and agreed upon to be till the death of one or the other? The Holy Scriptures rightly support this: 'For the woman which hath an husband is bound by the law to her husband so long as he liveth' (Romans 7. 2).

But what is Required of Thee, O Woman?

'Wilt thou have this man to thy wedded husband, to live together after God's ordinance in the holy estate of matrimony? Wilt thou obey him, and serve him, love, honour and keep him in sickness and in health; and, forsaking all other, keep thee only unto him so long as ye both shall live?' Yet again as this Marriage Service proceeds are all reminded of its weighty requirements; yet 'charity (or love) beareth all things' (1 Corinthians 13. 7).

Christian Marriage and Divorce

Wilt Thou Obey Him?

With regard to those who object to this question and prefer a substitute, we can either think that the question is not understood, or love is not deep enough. The example is very ancient: 'For after this manner in the old time the holy women also, who trusted in God, adorned themselves, being in subjection unto their own husbands: even as Sara obeyed Abraham, calling him lord (1 Peter 3. 5, 6; Genesis 18. 12). The Greek word used for 'obey' is HUPAKOUO meaning 'to hear under' (as a subordinate), i.e. to listen attentively; by implication 'to heed or conform to a command or authority; hearken; be obedient to; obey'. Those who are blessed with the grace of God and have the benefit of the new birth will perhaps feel better able to understand the meaning of the word 'obey' from the passage in Romans 6. 17 where the same Greek word is used: 'But God be thanked, that ye were the servants of sin, *but ye have obeyed from the heart* that form of doctrine that was delivered you.' We also find it in Hebrews 11. 8: 'By faith Abraham obeyed' (God).

It must ever be remembered that the basis of true and lasting marriage is founded on love for one another. The heart is the centre of our emotions; hence love is that to be accounted of in this obligation for the wife to obey her husband 'from the heart'. In the case of Abraham and Sarah it can be said that they loved God from the heart and in consequence their whole idea of obedience was regulated by the fear of the Lord in their hearts—what their Lord had said or indicated in their souls was their rule of life and no hardship was incurred by Sarah when she felt, in obeying her husband, she was obeying the command and authority of her God. This willingness on the part of the wife to obey is not to introduce servility to her husband. Let us go back to the original in Genesis: 'I will make him an help meet for him' (2.18). This point recognized by the husband should enable him to keep the relationship in a right perspective and love should rule and overrule all his actions and requests. Many husbands have lived long enough to thank God for the wife who has affectionately but faithfully pointed out the lack of wisdom in an action he proposed to take or a request that he made upon her; yet there was no question of her 'usurping authority over the man' (1 Timothy 2. 12). Paul reminds us in Ephesians 5. 33: 'Nevertheless let every one of you in particular so love his wife even as himself; and the wife see that she reverence her husband.' To the Christian wife or husband, a view of their all-glorious Lord willingly stooping to wash the disciples' feet and then saying, 'Ye call me Master and Lord: and ye say well; for so I am. If I then, your Lord and Master, have washed your feet; ye also ought to wash one another's feet. For I have given you an example, that you should do as I have done to you': this will put the spirit of both right and the love that filled their Saviour's heart, so that He humbled Himself, will affect theirs, though viewing the matter of obedience from opposite angles, especially when it is added, 'I am among you as one that serveth' (John 13. 13-15; Luke 22. 27).

The Nuptial Confessions and the Tying of the Bond

'Then the minister shall cause the man with his right hand to take the woman by her right hand, and to repeat after him: "I call upon these persons here present to witness that I, A– B–, do take thee, C– D–, to be my lawful wedded wife, to have and to hold from this day forward, for better for worse, for richer for poorer, in sickness and in health, to love and to cherish, till death us do part, according to God's holy ordinance; and thereto I plight thee my troth." ' The woman is then asked to repeat similar words. What love, what unreservedness, what complete unity of desire, what willingness to keep together under the most adverse and perverse conditions are expressed as the forcefulness of the words spoken reverberate through and thrill the very beings of the speakers and also those privileged to be witnesses on such an occasion!

What follows? As a practical token and continual reminder of the words spoken these words are pronounced after the minister: 'I give thee this ring in token of the vow and covenant now made betwixt me and thee, and in pledge of my affection and devotion.' Then the minister shall say: 'Forasmuch as A— B— and C— D— have consented together in holy wedlock, and have witnessed the same before God and this company, I pronounce them husband and wife, *in the name of the Father and of the Son and of the Holy Ghost.* And what God hath joined together, let not man put asunder. Amen.' Now the two enraptured people leave to commence a life together and to work out in practice what they have just professed.

CHAPTER 3

MARRIAGE AND ITS TRIALS

In the foregoing pages an attempt has been made to set forth the importance of marriage itself and the blessings of the married state. Those who have despised marriage and have thought it unnecessary, and in consequence have lived together in an unmarried state, often ultimately have found to their cost their mistake. Lack of security for the 'wife' may early be discovered when the 'husband' decides to change his mind and transfer his affections to another; too late the unmarried wife finds she has no legal redress. Again, in the 1939-45 war many who felt it was not worth while going through a boring ceremony suddenly realized that many difficulties arose regarding the obtaining of allowances which were given without question to the married. Though perhaps this may appear negative, yet the mention of it may well serve to emphasize the benefits that can and do accrue to those who are properly joined together. Let us always remember the blissful scene, and as an aid to this we would suggest the reading through of the vows taken on the wedding day each year, say, on the first day of the year or the wedding anniversary. What a reminder this may be of the happy day, and maybe the love felt and expressed at that time! Will this save a separation or divorce when the couple are feeling the frustrations of life with all its strains and tensions? It may well do. Will this revive something in the business-hardened husband reminding him that his marriage is to his wife and not to his business; she can return affection which his business has no power to give?

Christian Marriage and Divorce

It may well do. Will this bring a relief to the poor wife and mother, almost torn asunder by the tantrums and squabblings of her dear family, added to by the absent-mindedness of her husband who appears to lack appreciation of all her devoted efforts? It may well do.

Leaving this more mundane view of things, let us look at marriage in reality, and in its practical working out. May we expect to have reached the utopian state, heaven on earth, uninterrupted peace when the ring is put on the finger and the benediction is pronounced on the wedding day? Alas! if this is the pleasant picture (Isaiah 2. 16), how quickly those taught of the Spirit of God will have to prove that 'the loftiness of man shall be bowed down, and the haughtiness of men shall be made low: and the Lord alone shall be exalted in that day. And the idols he shall utterly abolish' (Isaiah 2. 17, 18). A honeymoon does not last long for there is soon a discovery by both that neither are angels but poor, fallen, depraved creatures, the subjects of passions, the victims of pride, and perhaps, to their utter astonishment at times, suspicion. Let the Christian pair always be aware of this, that what God has joined together, the devil will do his utmost to put asunder. This he does by working on the evil passions, exciting the pride of the heart, and becoming the 'whisperer that separateth chief friends' (Proverbs 16. 28), producing a suspicion that is but the child of suggestion. Let us quote from Colossians 3. 13: 'Forbearing one another and forgiving one another, if any man have a quarrel against any: even as Christ forgave you, so also do ye.' Listen to this word from the Lord and be not surprised then if you have to forbear, husband or wife; and forgive when a quarrel arises (sharp and short

Marriage and its Trials

though it may mercifully be). Whenever exhortations are given in the Scriptures, we should expect occasions to arise when such will be called into exercise. So beloved husband or wife, you will have to forbear (because God is blending two people into one), and sometimes forgive. The nearer you live to Christ in your daily walk and conversation, the easier you will find it to obey these requests.

But husbands, beware, be on your guard! Again from the same chapter we read 'Husbands love your wives, *and be not bitter against them.*' Can you conceive it on your wedding day? The Holy Bible speaketh not in vain. Again, as the husbands also become fathers, so a further warning is given: 'Fathers, provoke not your children to anger, lest they be discouraged.' A close personal cross-examination of your thoughts and actions by the grace of God will disclose that your children's anger has sometimes been justified and you have been responsible and guilty (Colossians 3. 21; Ephesians 6. 4).

'Wives, submit yourselves unto your own husbands, as it is fit in the Lord.' Is this exhortation really necessary? Surely the strong inference is that sometimes you will not be very willing to submit. Ponder the last few words, and may these produce a right spirit: 'as it is fit in the Lord'.

Sickness in the family, unexpected happenings when poverty may seem imminent, financial losses, family bereavements, self-sacrifice in order to provide for the children, adversities of various sorts, to say nothing of an internal conflict when one's own personal ego would exert itself and create havoc and distress in the family — these form some of the conditions which bring the marriage under trial. How many believers have found help and derived confidence as, according to their daily custom, together they have brought their troubles to their Lord at the family altar. In the trials arising every day, they prove that God not only joined them together in the first place but is now keeping them together when many circumstances around them would tear them apart. As they commit their way unto the Lord, so they trust His gracious promise: 'Many are the afflictions of the righteous, but the Lord delivereth him out of them all' (Psalm 34. 19).

Some readers may sigh and say their case is not like this: my husband is not with me in spiritual things or my wife is an atheist or an agnostic. Is it because you did not observe the exhortation, 'Be ye not unequally yoked with unbelievers' (2 Corinthians 6. 14) that this situation has arisen, that this 'rod for a fool's back' has fallen upon you (Proverbs 26. 3)? Or is it such a case that the Lord has called you by His grace since your wedding day so you are a changed person now, 'seeking first the kingdom of God and his righteousness' (Matthew 6. 33)? To such true believers we may say, 'But He giveth more grace' (James 4. 6).

We have therefore attempted to mention a few things in the life of a marriage which will give us some background when we come to consider the scriptural view on the matter of divorce and remarriage.

CHAPTER 4

DIVORCE

'This know also that in the last days perilous times shall come: for men shall be lovers of their own selves, covetous, boasters, proud, blasphemers, disobedient to parents, unthankful, unholy, without natural affection, trucebreakers, false accusers, incontinent, fierce, despisers of those that are good, traitors, heady, highminded, lovers of pleasures more than lovers of God' (2 Timothy 3. 1-4). Because of these prevailing conditions law and order to a large extent tends to be discarded and men are more and more becoming a law unto themselves; so we sadly see the rise in the divorce rate and a clamour for easier means of obtaining a separation. God and His Word change not even so, and it is our purpose now to investigate the voice of the Holy Bible in respect to this important subject that has been projected so prominently into everyday life. We shall first of all make quotations bearing upon the point.

What Jesus Christ Himself Said

1. 'The Pharisees also came unto him, tempting him, and saying unto him, Is it lawful for a man to put away his wife for every cause? And he answered and said unto them, Have ye not read, that he which made them at the beginning made them male and female, and said, For this cause shall a man leave father and mother, and shall cleave to his wife: and they twain shall be one flesh?

Wherefore they are no more twain, but one flesh.

Christian Marriage and Divorce

What therefore God hath joined together, let not man put asunder.

They say unto him, Why did Moses then command to give a writing of divorcement and to put her away? He saith unto them, Moses because of the hardness of your hearts suffered you to put away your wives: but from the beginning it was not so. And I say unto you, Whosoever shall put away his wife, except it be for fornication, and marry another, committeth adultery: and whoso marrieth her which is put away doth commit adultery' (Matthew 19. 3-9).

2. 'It hath been said, Whosoever shall put away his wife, let him give her a writing of divorcement: but I say unto you, That whosoever shall put away his wife, saving for the cause of fornication, causeth her to commit adultery: and whosoever shall marry her that is divorced committeth adultery' (Matthew 5. 31, 32).

3. 'And in the house his disciples asked him again of the same matter. And he saith unto them, Whosoever shall put away his wife, and marry another, committeth adultery against her. And if a woman shall put away her husband, and be married to another, she committeth adultery' (Mark 10. 10-12).

4. 'Whosoever putteth away his wife, and marrieth another, committeth adultery; and whosoever marrieth her that is put away from her husband committeth adultery' (Luke 16. 18).

Thus we have our Lord's pronouncement on this important subject, clear, decisive, and in consequence easily understood. But –

Divorce

What does Paul say in his Epistles under the Teaching and Inspiration of the Holy Spirit?

'For the woman which hath an husband is bound by the law to her husband so long as he liveth; but if the husband be dead, she is loosed from the law of her husband. So then if, while her husband liveth, she be married to another man, she shall be called an adulteress; but if her husband be dead, she is free from that law; so that she is no adulteress, though she be married to another man. Wherefore, my brethren, ye also are become dead to the law by the body of Christ; that ye should be married to another, even to him who is raised from the dead, that we should bring forth fruit unto God' (Romans 7. 2-4).

'And unto the married I command, yet not I, but the Lord, Let not the wife depart from her husband; but and if she depart, let her remain unmarried, or be reconciled to her husband; and let not the husband put away his wife' (1 Corinthians 7. 10, 11).

'For this cause shall a man leave his father and mother, and shall be joined unto his wife, and they two shall be one flesh. This is a great mystery; but I speak concerning Christ and the church. Nevertheless let every one of you in particular so love his wife even as himself; and the wife see that she reverence her husband' (Ephesians 5. 31-3).

How encouraging and how strengthening to our faith to find the New Testament speaking with one voice so that only the blindest of the blind cannot see and the deafest of the deaf cannot hear! Who are these? The proverb says: 'There are none so blind as those that won't see, and none so deaf as those that won't hear.' This is a common saying amongst the world in general.

Christian Marriage and Divorce

'Except (Saving) for Fornication'

These words are mentioned only in Matthew 5. 32 and 19. 9. In Mark and Luke no exception is mentioned. In Matthew 19. 9, as well as to a lesser degree in Matthew 5. 32, the context refers back to Deuteronomy 24. 1, 2: 'When a man hath taken a wife, and married her, and it come to pass that she find no favour in his eyes, because he hath found some uncleanness in her: then let him write her a bill of divorcement, and give it in her hand, and send her out of his house. And when she is departed out of his house she may go and be another man's wife.' The operative words in this quotation are 'some uncleanness', and it is not without some significance that the two Hebrew words used are only used with this sense on this occasion. The Hebrew word DABAR has a variety of meanings and 'some' is one, but only when related to uncleanness. For uncleanness the original word is ERVAH meaning, and translated elsewhere, 'disgrace, blemish, shame, nakedness'. It should be noted that the man who sought a bill of divorcement sought it at the very beginning of the association, he finding some uncleanness in her when he came to consummate the marriage. Under no circumstances can this Scripture be used to support divorce as it is currently understood today. A look at customs in Bible times will make this clear.

Betrothal and Marriage

In the days of our Lord a Jewish betrothal was particularly binding in character. It will be helpful to realize what is involved when a Hebrew or Oriental is married

Divorce

as this differs in many respects from our own customs. 'In the first place, the choice of the bride devolved, not on the bridegroom himself, but on his relations or on a friend deputed by the bridegroom for this purpose. The consent of the maiden was sometimes asked (Genesis 24. 58); but this appears to have been subordinate to the previous consent of the father and the adult brothers (Genesis 24. 51; 34. 11). Occasionally the whole business of selecting a wife was left in the hands of a friend. The selection of the bride was followed by the espousal, which was a formal proceeding, undertaken by a friend or legal representative on the part of the bridegroom and by the parents on the part of the bride: it was confirmed by oaths, and accompanied by giving presents to the bride. The act of betrothal was celebrated by a feast. Between the betrothal and the marriage an interval elapsed, varying from a few days in the patriarchal age (Genesis 24. 55) to a full year for virgins and a month for widows in later times. During this period the bride-elect lived with her friends and all communication between herself and her future husband was carried on through the medium of a friend deputed for the purpose, termed the "friend of the bridegroom" (John 3. 29). She was now virtually regarded as the wife of her future husband. Hence faithlessness on her part was punishable by death (Deuteronomy 22. 23, 24), the husband, however, having the option of "putting her away" (Matthew 1. 19 – as in the case of our Lord's mother and Joseph; Deuteronomy 24. 1). We now come to the wedding itself and in this the most observable point is that there were no definite religious ceremonies connected with it. It is probable, indeed, that some formal ratification of the espousal with an oath took place as implied in some allusions to marriage but the essence of the marriage ceremony consisted in the removal of the bride from her father's house to that of the bridegroom or his father' (*A Smaller Dictionary of the Bible*, by William Smith, DCL, LLD).

This is the light in which the opening verses of Deuteronomy 24 should be seen and not, as some seem to do, make it an excuse to support their views on divorce, on the grounds of adultery which occurs perhaps long after the marriage has been consummated.

The Meaning of Matthew 5. 32 and 19. 9

The Lord confirmed the sacred and lasting character of marriage (Matthew 19. 4-8). What was His meaning in saying there could be no 'putting away' of a wife 'except for fornication'? We have seen that it is clearly linked to the background of Deuteronomy 24—well known to His audience. In the original Greek, the word translated 'fornication' is PORNEIA, which is a word that often has a wide meaning of 'sexual immorality, prostitution and impure practices generally'. Scriptural examples are Acts 15. 20, 29; 1 Corinthians 6. 13, 18; Colossians 3. 5; and there are others. The word is often translated 'fornication', by which is generally understood 'improper relations while unmarried', as distinct from 'adultery' meaning 'improper relations *after* marriage'. The Greek word for 'adultery' is MOICHEIA and this is always so translated, as it is in the latter part of Matthew 19. 9. It seems evident that, in making the exception, the Lord did not mean 'adultery'—otherwise, surely, He would have used the same word as later in the verse. (There

Divorce

are other passages of Scripture where both words occur and 'fornication' clearly means something other than 'adultery': e.g. Matthew 15. 19; Mark 7. 21; 1 Corinthians 6. 9; Galatians 5. 19.) What did the Lord mean? *In the context in which He was speaking* it seems clear that He was certainly not referring to adultery, nor to the broad range of sins such as prostitution, but simply to impurity before marriage. Thus these texts in Matthew do not provide grounds for divorce because of adultery as is commonly asserted. Such an assertion opens wide the floodgates for divorce, and is in any event utterly contrary to the pure standards of marriage upheld by the Lord Jesus: 'From the beginning it was not so' (Matthew 19. 8).

Adultery in the Sight of God

The thoughtless multitudes in our own land never consider that adultery is a sin against God; nor do many that profess to be governed by Christian principles. The Holy Bible speaks with a clear voice. From Genesis 20 we read of Sarah saying that she was Abraham's sister and that Abimelech, King of Gerar, sent and took her. 'But God came to Abimelech in a dream by night and said to him, Behold, thou art but a dead man, for the woman which thou hast taken; for she is a man's wife....' Then in verse 6 we read: 'And God said unto him in a dream, Yea, I know that thou didst this in the integrity of thy heart; for I also withheld thee from *sinning against me*: therefore suffered I thee not to touch her.' When King David was guilty of adultery with Bathsheba he says to Nathan the prophet, 'I have sinned *against the Lord*', which is further emphasized in his penitential Psalm: 'Against thee, thee only, have I sinned and done this evil in thy sight: that thou mightest be justified when thou speakest, and be clear when thou judgest' (2 Samuel 12. 13; Psalm 51. 4).

Clear Conclusions from the New Testament

1. 'They twain shall be one flesh.'

2. 'Moses because of the hardness of your hearts suffered you to put away your wives: *but from the beginning it was not so.*'

3. 'Whosoever shall put away his wife, except it be for fornication, and marrieth another, *committeth adultery*.' The point concerning fornication has already been covered. Because there is in this country, compared with Bible times and places, no betrothal of such a nature and subsequent marriage, it can hardly be pleaded that fornication can be used as an excuse for divorce. Our nearest approach to betrothal and marriage is what is called the 'engagement' period. No marriage takes place until the end of that period so, even if fornication should take place, it affords no excuse since a marriage cannot be broken up which has not begun. As a result we must reaffirm that the words of the Lord Jesus, 'except it be for fornication', have no relevance to the present-day situation.

4. 'And whoso marrieth her which is put away *doth commit adultery*.'

5. 'And if a woman shall put away her husband and be married to another, *she committeth adultery*.'

6. 'For the woman which hath an husband is *bound* by the law to her husband as long as he liveth.'

Divorce

7. 'But if her husband be dead, she is at liberty to be married to whom she will' (1 Corinthians 7. 39). 'She is loosed from the law of her husband.'

8. 'So then if, while her husband liveth, she be married to another man, she shall be called an adulteress.'

9. 'Let not the wife depart from her husband.'

10. 'But if she depart, let her remain *unmarried*, or be reconciled to her husband.'

11. 'Let not the husband put away his wife.'

The teaching of the Holy Scriptures is clear—once the marriage bond has been sealed, nothing but death can destroy it. Intolerable atmospheres may cause one to depart but under no consideration must that person marry again whilst the other party is alive. This teaching is binding on every true believer. The world at large—the ungodly, the infidel, the agnostic, the rejector of the Word of God, etc., may refuse to accept it; the law of the land may allow the opposite; but the true believer, regulated by the fear of the Lord and love to his Lord and his Lord's words, will have to say, 'Let God be true, but every man a liar' (Romans 3. 4).

'Let Him/Her Depart'

'But to the rest speak I, not the Lord: if any brother hath a wife that believeth not, and she be pleased to dwell with him, let him not put her away. And the woman which hath an husband that believeth not, and if he be pleased to dwell with her, let her not leave him. For the unbelieving husband is sanctified by the wife, and the unbelieving wife is sanctified by the husband:

else were your children unclean; but now are they holy. But if the unbelieving depart, let him depart. A brother or a sister is not under bondage in such cases: but God hath called us to peace. For what knowest thou, O wife, whether thou shalt save thy husband? or how knowest thou, O man, whether thou shalt save thy wife?' (1 Corinthians 7. 12-16).

The Apostle Paul's arrival in Corinth is described to us in Acts chapter 18. It appears that what Paul saw there troubled him and filled him with some fear for we find the Lord spoke to him: 'Then spake the Lord to Paul in the night by a vision, Be not afraid, but speak, and hold not thy peace; for I am with thee, and no man shall set on thee to hurt thee; for I have much people in this city.' When the gospel is preached in a city given up to ungodliness and all wickedness, it may follow, and does follow, that 'some believed and some believed not'. This at times affected households and brought about the situation which Paul speaks about. Where a man and woman know nothing of Christian teaching, then their relationship can never rise above the natural. Now through the preaching of Paul the wife believes, the husband does not; the husband believes, the wife does not: one has changed; the other has not—'This is not the man/woman I married', will be the cry of the unbelieving one. Must the believer go? Must the unbeliever be cast out of the household? No, a thousand times no. If both are willing to live together still, then who can tell but that in time, by the quiet example of the believer, the other party might also become a believer and enjoy not only the benefit of the natural bond but also of a spiritual bond?

However, suppose the breach is so great now, the

Divorce

unbeliever's enmity being so deep and venting all its spleen, that the person that was so much loved has become the object of bitter hatred, what then? 'But if the unbelieving depart, let him depart. A brother or a sister is not under bondage in such cases.' What does this mean? Is this person now free to break the marriage union and assume it to be concluded, he or she now possessing a palpable case for divorce? The unbeliever may think so, but this the believer cannot accept. The unbeliever is not bound to stay in such cases, but it must ever be remembered that the Scriptures cannot be broken as far as the truth is concerned. 'But and if she depart, let her remain unmarried.' Hence the bondage the apostle refers to, and one's freedom from under it, is restricted to departing and not extended to include the forgetting of the marriage vows and the tearing up of the marriage lines. At the same time, the believer is not under bondage to try to get the unbeliever back at all costs. 'But to the rest speak I, not the Lord': Paul here is not expressing his personal opinion. His other writings were based on what was written in the Scriptures already; now a new situation has arisen not referred to in the Holy Bible before. In this sense, he says: 'Not the Lord.' Nevertheless, what is written is based on the analogy of Holy Writ and the inferences drawn accordingly. These words are still to be regarded as amongst the 'inspired writings'.

CHAPTER 5

CHRIST OUR EXAMPLE

Having read so far, have some come to the conclusion that the theory is good but can this really be reduced to practice? There are many things which our flesh finds irksome, but grace and faith being given, still enables one to perform. We shall now touch a high spiritual plane about which some readers may say, 'It is beyond me. I cannot attain unto it'; whilst others may appreciate its deeper spiritual value. To those who feel the chapter is beyond their reach, maybe in a few years' time, when their Christian experience has broadened, they will enjoy reading it. The whole basis of the marriage union and its maintenance is set before us in its highest degree and greatest glory when we consider Christ and His church. 'Even as Christ also loved the church, and gave himself for it' (Ephesians 5. 25). Further down in the same chapter we read: 'But I speak concerning Christ and the church' (verse 32). Shall the Bride of Christ—those many persons throughout the ages who are blessed with the fear of the Lord, quickened by the Holy Spirit, made partakers of the divine nature—view marriage, holy matrimony, on any lesser plane than the perfect bond that exists between her Beloved and herself? But what about the behaviour of the Bride, who is made to feel so keenly the power of indwelling sin: what of the backsliding spirit, whether internal or external sometimes; the waywardness and wantonness; the desire to consider self first in so many things; the inward rebellion against Christ's rule? Is this the Bride of Christ, so apparently

Christ our Example

defiled? It is her carnal side that the Holy Bible describes: 'Because the carnal mind is enmity against God; for it is not subject to the law of God, neither indeed can be. So then they that are in the flesh cannot please God' (Romans 8. 7, 8).

Is there another side to this person then? There is. 'But ye are not in the flesh, but in the Spirit, if so be that the Spirit of God dwell in you' (Romans 8. 9). This is the spiritual side capable of being engaged in a spiritual bond with Christ. Hence this true nature of the Bride of Christ sighs, grieves, repents, sorrows over her unbecoming behaviour to her lovely Husband. She has found Him to be so forbearing, forgiving, understanding, patient, compassionate, longsuffering, and so full of love that covers all sins (Proverbs 10. 12). Yes, she remembers that it was not just a covering of the moment but an eternal covering occasioned by His laying down His life to atone for her wretchedness and to wash away all the stains as well. 'Greater love hath no man than this, that a man lay down his life for his friends' (John 15. 13). Hear her conclusion in the Song of Solomon: 'His mouth is most sweet; yea, he is altogether lovely. This is my beloved, and this is my friend, O daughters of Jerusalem' (5. 16). Amongst other things what were the precious words that she heard? 'For the Lord, the God of Israel, saith that he hateth putting away' (Malachi 2. 16). If sometimes the Bride has felt separation—'But your iniquities have separated between you and your God, and your sins have hid his face from you that he will not hear' (Isaiah 59. 2), yet there is no question of divorce. The call is always there: 'Even from the days of your fathers ye are gone away from mine ordinances, and have not kept them. Return unto me, and I will return unto you, saith the Lord of hosts' (Malachi 3. 7).

O believer, beloved, with the love of your Husband in your soul, now overwhelmed by His lovingkindness in not even mentioning putting you away when you knew you deserved to be; will you now say, 'I cannot put up with my wife's/my husband's behaviour any longer'?

> Could we bear from one another
> What He daily bears from us?
>
> His is love beyond a brother's—
> Costly, free and knows no end;
> They who once his kindness prove,
> Find it everlasting love.

Love is not represented merely by what may well prove to be nothing more than lustful desire; love has to be proved, has to undergo hardships, endure good report and also evil report, be rejoiced in in health but no less in sickness. Let us profitably take to our heart the voice of the Holy Bible in the well-known passage from 1 Corinthians 13: 'Charity suffereth long and is kind; charity envieth not; charity vaunteth not itself, is not puffed up, doth not behave itself unseemly, seeketh not her own, is not easily provoked, thinketh no evil; rejoiceth not in iniquity, but rejoiceth in the truth; beareth all things, believeth all things, hopeth all things, endureth all things. Charity never faileth.' 'Weak in myself, in Him I'm strong.' 'I can do all things through Christ that strengtheneth me' (Philippians 4. 13).

There is the story of the gathering of Scottish ministers when each one was to speak on the subject of: 'How has your wife benefited you in your ministry?' All present

Christ our Example

knew that one of their brethren had a wife who had treated him very badly, making him live under much privation and very trying conditions. As one after another was able to tell how good and helpful their wives had been, kind and thoughtful in every way and so on, the underlying thoughts of all were concentrated on the speculation as to what their poor, despised, persecuted brother would say. Eventually the minister's turn came and all ears hung upon his words. He said, 'My brethren, you have all spoken of the benefit your wives have been to you but none of your wives has sent you to the throne of grace as often as mine has to plead for mercy, to seek for help and strength to endure, and see Him who is invisible in the process.' He never even thought of divorce because his poor, persecuting wife was a means God used to keep his soul lively and to bring him to have closer union and communion with his blessed Lord and Saviour.

Come then, any who may read this and be under the temptation at the time to separate because the partner is so troublesome, so tantalizing, so trying; will you, can you think of putting away when you know that you have been just as troublesome, tantalizing, and trying to your best Beloved? And He has not cast you off. Yea He has said, 'I have chosen thee and not cast thee away' (Isaiah 41. 9). When Christ sheds abroad His love in your hearts by the Holy Ghost, surely His example you must follow for, 'Charity shall cover the multitude of sins' (1 Peter 4. 8).

What a victory has been gained for love and by love! The believer is blessed with an enduring love to Christ which will again and again focus on the words in the

Christian Marriage and Divorce

Lamentations of Jeremiah: 'Is it nothing to you, all ye that pass by? Behold, and see if there be any sorrow like unto my sorrow, which is done unto me, wherewith the Lord hath afflicted me in the day of his fierce anger' (1. 12). A glimpse of Christ's sufferings will often make the believing husband or wife say:

> His way was much rougher and darker than mine;
> Did Christ my Lord suffer and shall I repine?

CHAPTER 6

CHURCH MEMBERSHIP

Because of the perilous times in which we now live, carnal views, the outcome of modern theology(?), have cast aside the Holy Scriptures and superseded them with humanistic ideas and worldly conformity. Instead of clarifying truth that was already clear to the spiritual and discerning, these have introduced confusion. Many who may tend to go along with these new and liberal propositions also have an uneasy feeling inside as to their rightness. With respect to divorced persons who were living together being accepted for or retaining church membership, less than half a century ago the very thought in many quarters would neither have been countenanced nor tolerated. But times have changed, not for the better but for the worse. Alas! we now discover without effort that a large number of churches of all denominations are willing to circumvent the Holy Scriptures in order to satisfy the ungodly tastes of their carnalized 'Christians'—carnalized church members. The Lord Jesus in his sermon on the mount makes it clear that, 'Ye cannot serve God and mammon' (Matthew 6. 24).

Therefore can an Adulterer or Adulteress be or remain a Church Member?

'Know ye not that the unrighteous shall not inherit the kingdom of God? Be not deceived: neither fornicators, nor idolaters, nor adulterers, nor effeminate, nor abusers

Christian Marriage and Divorce

of themselves with mankind, nor thieves, nor covetous, nor drunkards, nor revilers, nor extortioners, shall inherit the kingdom of God' (1 Corinthians 6. 9, 10). Since then such persons, living and dying so, cannot be heirs in the end, how can they be church members, or be allowed to continue as church members, when their very behaviour speaks loudly against them? Reading further in the same chapter: 'Know ye not that your bodies are the members of Christ? shall I then take the members of Christ, and make them the members of an harlot? God forbid. What? know ye not that he which is joined to an harlot is one body? for two, saith he, shall be one flesh. But he that is joined unto the Lord is one spirit.'

That many if not all of the members of Christ's body, the church, have been sadly guilty of the crimes listed is undoubted; if not in the outward act, in the inward lust these have been committed. Let us hear the voice of the Holy Bible: 'And such were some of you: but ye are washed, but ye are sanctified, but ye are justified in the name of the Lord Jesus, and by the Spirit of our God.' Let all true Christians, born again of the Spirit, made partakers of the divine nature, give their own verdict. Are you washed in the fountain opened for sin and for uncleanness (Zechariah 13. 1)? Are you sanctified unto holiness, having been made 'meet to be partakers of the inheritance of the saints in light: who hath delivered us from the power of darkness, and hath translated us into the kingdom of his dear Son' (Colossians 1. 12-13)? Are you justified freely by His grace (Titus 3. 7)? Then can you 'continue in sin that grace may abound? God forbid', says the Apostle Paul. 'How shall we, that are dead to sin, live any longer therein?' (Romans 6. 1, 2). There can only be one answer, NO.

Church Membership

A person who shall put away his wife and marrieth another committeth adultery; whoso marrieth her that is put away committeth adultery; the woman that shall put away her husband and be married to another, she committeth adultery: the result in each case, living in sin. This is the testimony of the Holy Scriptures. In the Book of Exodus the moral law sounds loud and long: 'Thou shalt not commit adultery' (20. 14). Shall a member of a Christian church flagrantly ignore this command of the Almighty God and still remain in membership? Shall such a person or persons be so blind as not to see their hypocrisy in carrying on a relationship which is contrary to God's Word and yet have the effrontery to say they love the Lord and love to keep His commandments? There is only one answer that honours God and that is that such a person or persons shall not be accepted for or remain in membership of a Christian church—

Unless

there is repentance and fruits unto repentance brought forth. Sin cannot be repented of until a person is convicted and convinced of it. Who can convince even though one might convict? Even though what may seem to be unanswerable arguments may be pressed, yet, as the worldly proverb says: 'A man convinced against his will is of the same opinion still.' It will not do for a person to repent with the lips only; repentance must be from the heart and confession must be clear, definite, and unqualified: 'I was wrong; I am wrong; I feel I am wrong; I know I am wrong; this must be put right in the sight of God.'

Are there any difficulties to such a repentance? Indeed there are. How loudly will the opposing flesh contest the issue! You cannot leave your 'wife'; you cannot leave your 'husband'; look how happy you have been, and what about the children, what will they do? There is but one answer, the outcome of God's work who has said, 'For with God nothing shall be impossible' (Luke 1. 37). Let us hear His own words: 'If any man come to me and hate not his father, and mother, and wife, and children, and brethren, and sisters, yea and his own life also, he cannot be my disciple'—unless he obeys Me first whatever it may cost, whatever privations may result, whatever heart rendings may transpire, then he cannot be My disciple.

Do you say; 'But God is love, He cannot be so hard?' 'He hath showed thee, O man, what is good: and what doth the Lord require of thee, but to do justly, and to love mercy, and to walk humbly with thy God?' (Micah 6. 8). Have you done justly or/and acted mercifully or/and walked humbly with your God when He says, 'They two shall be one flesh', when you have put away your wife, your husband? Can you say that you have lived happily together when the foundation of your marriage has been built on the misery of a deserted wife or husband? If you are God's child, you must be chastised and His chastisement is for your profit. So if the Almighty God convinces an adulterer or adulteress of their sin, such will not have to be argued with for the Lord Himself will have shown them the wrongfulness of their case. They will haste to do that which is right in the sight of God.

Church Membership

The Case of the Man or Woman Deserted

A husband or wife may indeed be left, the opposite number having engaged in some adulterous association with another and, not having the grace of God, sued for and obtained a divorce. If the innocent party remains upright in life and enters no other association with a member of the opposite sex, then there is no question of anything having been done that would warrant any action by the church except to show deep sympathy for the person so treated. Should the adulterous party eventually die, then and only then would the innocent party be free to marry again. Such actions would not be contrary to the Lord's commandments and therefore the person concerned would be welcome to the Lord's table according to church order.

An Unusual Case

In February 1853 a question was put to the then editor of the *Gospel Standard* as follows: 'A married female was deserted by her husband. After the lapse of thirteen years she marries again, supposing her husband was dead; but after six or seven years time the first husband returns. Can this female consistently continue a member of a gospel church?'

In 1853 communications were very different from what they are today, and in this sense the case could be considered irrelevant. It does, though, bring us back to a basic question as to whether a church should allow a woman/man to continue in church membership who has married a second time in the lifetime of the first husband/wife. We quote from the answer to the above question when the editor gives

Christian Marriage and Divorce

Five Good Reasons for the Church to say 'No'

1. It is evidently, as we have shown, unscriptural for a woman/man to marry a second husband/wife in the lifetime of the first. In the case before us the husband's long absence and her consequent belief of his death, though they diminish her guilt in remarrying, do not disannul her first marriage. By allowing her, therefore, to continue in church membership the church would sanction what is forbidden by the laws of God.

2. It would open the mouth of the world, always ready enough to spy out inconsistencies. A church is bound by the strongest motives to put away every stumbling block and cause of reproach. Though not mentioned, yet it seems almost implied that the woman is still living with the second husband. If this were sanctioned by the church, would it not justly be a matter of reproach?

3. It would probably be the source of perpetual strife and heart-burning, as it is evident the circumstance has already much tried the minds of the church and become a question of dispute amongst them.

4. It would rob some, if not many, of the members of all comfort and profit at the communion table, even if their views were not fully decided on the point; as we well know that when the mind is tossed up and down with doubts and suspicions, there is little but disquietude at the Lord's Supper.

5. If the poor woman be of a tender conscience, it might lead hereafter, if not now, to much distress of mind lest she should have received the Lord's Supper to her own condemnation.

Church Membership

We may repeat that though discipline has to be taken, this does not mean that such a person will never be received back again into church fellowship. In 1 Corinthians 5 the Apostle Paul directs the church to 'put him away from among yourselves', that is, separate him from church fellowship. Such a person is not to be forgotten by the other members of the church but these are to pray for his repentance and hope for his return with a chastened spirit and manifesting 'fruits meet for repentance'. When this is seen, then in 2 Corinthians 2. 6-8 we read: 'Sufficient to such a man is this punishment, which was inflicted of many. So that contrariwise ye ought rather to forgive him, and comfort him, lest perhaps such a one should be swallowed up with overmuch sorrow. Wherefore I beseech you that ye would confirm your love toward him.' Can we believe that he continued afterwards to live with her? Would he not, as a proof of his repentance, put her away and continue to live separately from her? When the Lord Jesus said to the woman taken in the very act of adultery by the Pharisees, 'Neither do I condemn thee; go and sin no more', can any conceive that she did other than take all the steps necessary to cease from that way of sinning, whatever it may have cost her and however much she may have been inconvenienced? 'The love of Christ constraineth us' would rule and reign in both cases. 'There is joy in heaven over one sinner that repenteth.' Will it not be so in the church of God on earth?

The Position of Pastors, Ministers, Elders, and Deacons

'A bishop then must be blameless, *the husband of one wife*, vigilant, sober, of good behaviour, given to

Christian Marriage and Divorce

hospitality. . . .' 'Let the deacons be husbands of one wife, ruling their children and their own houses well.' 'For this cause left I thee in Crete, that thou shouldest set in order the things that are wanting, and ordain elders in every city, as I had appointed thee: if any be blameless, the husband of one wife . . .' (1 Timothy 3. 2, 12; Titus 1. 5, 6). Some may say that such warnings and directions refer to polygamy but the point is now made that this refers also, if not more particularly, to a person who is divorced and has two 'wives' living. It should be remembered that in law a divorced man has to pay alimony to his separated wife so that though there is a separation, there still remains a recognition of the original tie. The position is clear: no man that is divorced and remarries may hold the position of pastor, minister, elder, or deacon in any church. This is the voice of the Holy Scriptures.

CHAPTER 7

IN CONCLUSION

'The weapons of our warfare are not carnal' (2 Corinthians 10. 4) but no doubt some readers of this booklet, finding it as 'the axe is laid unto the root' (Matthew 3. 10) will rise up with their carnal weapons in an attempt to destroy or smother over the truth that has been set forth. We know that various commentators have expressed quite different views in their interpretations. Whilst we make no pretension to being a voice crying in the wilderness in the latter day, yet we do say that we are not called to follow men, even good men if their views depart from the Scriptures. We are satisfied that the Almighty God knows what purposes are to be performed in sending forth this treatise and we are content to leave it in His hand to send it forth and preserve it until the blessing He may command has been accomplished. If it is useful in clearing gracious people's minds, establishing the truth concerning this important matter in the churches of Christ, and recovering some from the error of their ways, in each bringing glory to God, then we shall be more than recompensed for the labour and spiritual exercise that has been involved in producing it.